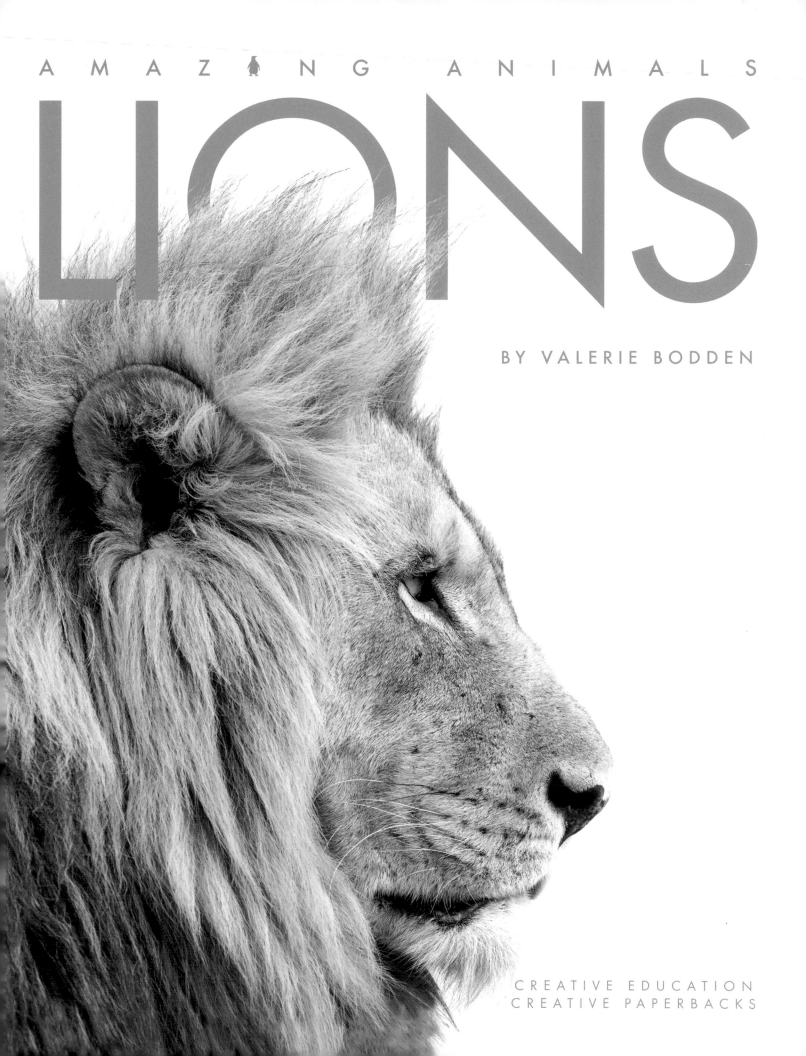

AMAZING ANIMALS

# LIONS

BY VALERIE BODDEN

CREATIVE EDUCATION
CREATIVE PAPERBACKS

Published by Creative Education and
Creative Paperbacks
P.O. Box 227, Mankato, Minnesota 56002
Creative Education and Creative Paperbacks are
imprints of The Creative Company
www.thecreativecompany.us

Design by The Design Lab
Production by Angela Korte and Colin O'Dea
Art direction by Rita Marshall
Printed in the United States of America

Photographs by Corbis (Norbert Wu), Getty
Images (busypix/iStock, Neale Howarth/500px,
Stan Osolinski, Panoramic Images, RobHainer/
Stoc...rieHolding/iStock, Valerie Shaff, Anup
Shah, Paul Souders, Art Wolfe), iStockphoto (Eric
sselee, Dani Kristiani, lrosebrugh), Shutterstock (Papa
Bravo)

Library of Congress Cataloging-in-Publication Data
Names: Bodden, Valerie, author.
Title: Lions / Valerie Bodden.
Series: Amazing animals.
Includes bibliographical references and index.
Summary: This revised edition surveys key aspects of
lions, describing the roaring big cats' appearance,
behaviors, and habitats. A folk tale explains why
these creatures are known as the king of the animals.
Identifiers: ISBN 978-1-64026-206-5 (hardcover)
/ ISBN 978-1-62832-769-4 (pbk) / ISBN 978-1-
54000-331-6 (eBook)
This title has been submitted for CIP processing under
LCCN 2019937911.

CCSS: RI.1.1, 2, 4, 5, 6, 7; RI.2.2, 5, 6, 7, 10;
RI.3.1, 5, 7, 8; RF.1.1, 3, 4; RF.2.3, 4

First Edition HC 9 8 7 6 5 4 3 2 1
First Edition PBK 9 8 7 6 5 4 3 2 1

# Table of Contents

# Lions are big cats. They live in hot places. Lions are the second-largest cats in the world. Only tigers grow bigger than lions.

*Lions live in family groups called prides.*

# Lions are strong. They are covered with golden fur. Lions have big teeth and sharp claws. Male lions have a mane. This is the bushy hair around the male's head and neck. Manes range in color from yellow to black.

*Lions' tails can be nearly half the length of their bodies.*

Male lions are about eight feet (2.4 m) long. They weigh more than two grown-up men put together! Female lions are a little smaller. Male lions are stronger, but females are faster. They can sprint up to 50 miles (80.5 km) per hour.

*Males with darker manes are stronger than those with lighter manes.*

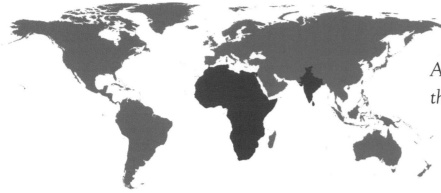

*Asiatic lions are smaller than African lions.*

Most lions live on the **continent** of Africa. Many live on **savannas**. Others live in dry forests. About 500 lions live in India. They are called Asiatic (*ay-zhe-AT-ick*) lions.

**continent**  one of Earth's seven big pieces of land

**savannas**  grassy areas with few trees

Lions hunt other animals. Some animals that lions hunt are zebras, wildebeest, and antelopes. Lions usually eat less than 20 pounds (9.1 kg) of meat in a day. But they can eat more than 55 pounds (24.9 kg) at once.

*After a large meal, lions will not eat for two or three days.*

*A group of baby lions born together is called a litter.*

A lion has up to six **cubs** at a time. At first, the cubs drink milk from their mother. When they are about five weeks old, they begin to eat meat. Most female lions stay with their mother's pride. Males leave the pride after two to four years. Lions in the wild can live about 15 years.

**cubs**  baby lions

# Lions can easily overheat. Some climb trees to avoid sunlight and biting flies. Lions sleep and rest about 20 hours a day. Cubs spend a lot of time playing. This play helps cubs learn how to hunt.

*A pride may have about 3 to 40 members.*

# Lions move around the most at night. Sometimes they roar. This roar can be heard five miles (8 km) away. Lions often hunt at night. They work together as a team.

*Female lions do most of the hunting for the pride.*

# Today, some people go to Africa to see lions in the wild. Others travel to India. It is exciting to see these big, furry cats up-close!

*Male lions watch over cubs while lionesses hunt.*

*A Lion Tale*

# Long ago, the animals of the forest gathered. They wanted a leader to protect them. The old ape was put in charge of the election. Suddenly, an earthquake shook the ground. Big rocks trapped the ape. No one could move the rocks without hurting the ape. But then the lion tried. He was strong and smart. He figured out how to move the rocks. The ape was saved! Then the lion was named king.

# Read More

Gagne, Tammy. *Lions: Built for the Hunt.* North Mankato, Minn.: Capstone Press, 2016.

Marsh, Laura. *Lions.* Washington, D.C.: National Geographic, 2015.

Meister, Cari. *Do You Really Want to Meet a Lion?* North Mankato, Minn.: Amicus, 2016.

# Websites

Easy Science for Kids: Lions—The Big Cats
*https://easyscienceforkids.com/all-about-lions/*
Watch a video about lions and read more about these big cats.

Enchanted Learning: Lions
*https://www.enchantedlearning.com/subjects/mammals/lion/coloring.shtml*
This site has lion facts and a picture to color.

National Geographic Kids: Lions
*https://kids.nationalgeographic.com/animals/lion*
Read more about lions, watch videos, and take a quiz about big cats!

Note: Every effort has been made to ensure that the websites listed above are suitable for children, that they have educational value, and that they contain no inappropriate material. However, because of the nature of the Internet, it is impossible to guarantee that these sites will remain active indefinitely or that their contents will not be altered.

# Index